A Deeper Motivation Beyond A Salary

How to Thrive in Work and Life.

Table of Content

Introduction: The Balancing Act of Work and Life 3

Chapter 1: When Influences Impact Upon Work Motivation 4

Chapter 2: Well-being Within the Workplace 9

Chapter 3: A Journey to Purpose and Fulfillment 15

Chapter 4: An Obsession with Being Busy 20

Chapter 5: Seeing the Journey Ahead of the Crossroad 25

Chapter 6: Beyond the Salary: What Would Get You Out of Bed at 4 a.m.? 31

Chapter 7: The Art of Switching Off 37

Chapter 8: Lived Experiences Can Widen the Perspective 43

Conclusion: Designing Your Future on Your Own Terms 49

Introduction: The Balancing Act of Work and Life

In today's world, the line between work and life has become blurred. Many of us struggle to leave work behind when we go home, often feeling overwhelmed by the constant demands of our jobs. This struggle manifests in various ways: stress, a lack of time for ourselves or loved ones, and even losing touch with the things that bring us happiness outside of work.

This book explores how the challenges of work can affect our ability to enjoy life beyond the workplace. Some of these effects are negative—like stress or burnout—while others are positive, such as the sense of purpose and fulfillment that can come from meaningful work.

No matter where you are in your career—whether you're just starting out or further along—you'll likely face the same core issues: balancing your time, managing stress, and finding joy both at work and outside of it. This book takes a deep dive into these themes, offering practical advice and real-life examples to help you manage your own work-life balance.

Chapter 1: When Influences Impact Upon Work Motivation

Ask yourself this: do you come home from work each day feeling energised and happy? Or do you feel drained and stressed, with little energy left for the things you truly enjoy? For many, the answer comes quickly—and it's often negative. Whether we realize it or not, our jobs significantly affect how we feel, both physically and mentally. Work can be a source of growth and fulfillment, driving us to achieve more and improve ourselves. But when work environments become toxic, stressful, or uninspiring, the same job that once motivated us can start to feel like a burden, sapping our enthusiasm and draining our energy.

Workplace motivation is shaped by a combination of factors—some internal and others external. We can break these down into two categories: external factors (such as salary, recognition, leadership, and company culture) and intrinsic motivation (the personal drive and values that inspire us to do our best). Both play a major role in how we feel about our jobs, and understanding this balance can help us navigate the ups and downs of working life.

External Factors That Influence Work Motivation

External factors are often the first things that come to mind when we think about job satisfaction. Things like salary, job perks, and company benefits all have an immediate impact on how we feel about our work. After all, it's hard to be motivated when you feel underpaid or unappreciated.

1. **Salary and Benefits**
   It's no secret that people work to earn a living. Having a decent salary is crucial because it meets our basic

needs—food, housing, and financial security. However, studies have shown that once people earn enough to cover their essential needs, money alone doesn't bring long-term motivation. For example, if you're earning a good salary but working in a toxic environment where you feel undervalued, that paycheque won't keep you happy for long. On the other hand, a job that offers a lower salary but comes with personal growth opportunities, supportive colleagues, or flexible hours may bring more satisfaction in the long run.

2. **Leadership and Company Culture**
Leadership plays a critical role in shaping the work environment. A good leader can inspire, motivate, and support their employees, creating a positive atmosphere where people feel valued. A toxic or unsupportive leader, on the other hand, can do just the opposite. Poor leadership can lead to high levels of stress, burnout, and a lack of motivation across the team. Similarly, company culture—the shared values, attitudes, and practices within an organisation—impacts how employees feel about their workplace. A culture that promotes collaboration, respect, and inclusion will naturally motivate people more than one that is cutthroat or overly competitive.

3. **Recognition and Reward**
Everyone wants to feel recognised for their hard work. It's human nature to seek acknowledgment for the effort we put into something, especially at work. Recognition doesn't always have to be in the form of bonuses or raises, although those are certainly appreciated. Even a simple "thank you" or public acknowledgment of a job well done can go a long way in keeping employees motivated. Many companies have

started to understand the value of creating reward systems that go beyond monetary compensation, offering programs for employee recognition that focus on personal achievements, milestones, and teamwork.

Intrinsic Motivation: The Personal Drive That Keeps Us Going

While external factors like salary and recognition are important, they are only part of the picture. The real, lasting motivation comes from within. Intrinsic motivation is about doing something because you find it rewarding, meaningful, or fulfilling—not just because you're being paid to do it.

1. **Meaningful Work**
   Many of us spend a large part of our lives working, so it's only natural to want that time to feel purposeful. Meaningful work is a key driver of intrinsic motivation. When our job aligns with our values, interests, and beliefs, it feels more rewarding. We are more likely to be engaged and committed to our work when we know it has a purpose beyond just a paycheck. For example, someone who is passionate about helping others may feel more fulfilled working in healthcare or social services, where they can make a direct impact on people's lives. When work has meaning, it doesn't feel like a chore—it feels like a mission.

Unfortunately, many people end up in jobs that don't align with their passions or values. They may have taken a job out of necessity, convenience, or because it was the "safe" choice. Over time, this can lead to frustration and a lack of motivation. However, it's never too late to find or create meaning in your work. Whether it's through seeking out projects that you're passionate about or finding ways to make your current job more aligned with your values, creating meaning at work is crucial for long-term motivation and satisfaction.

2. **Personal Growth and Development**
   Another key element of intrinsic motivation is the opportunity for growth and learning. When a job offers room for personal development, employees are more likely to stay engaged and motivated. Continuous learning allows us to improve our skills, gain new knowledge, and feel a sense of progress. This doesn't necessarily mean getting promoted or climbing the corporate ladder, although that can be part of it. It's about feeling challenged in a way that helps us grow, both personally and professionally.

Companies that invest in their employees' development are more likely to retain motivated staff. Offering training programs, workshops, and opportunities for advancement shows employees that the company values their growth. On the flip side, a job that feels stagnant, where there is no room for learning or advancement, can quickly lead to disengagement. Even if a person enjoys their work, doing the same thing every day without any challenge or growth can make the job feel monotonous.

3. **Autonomy and Control**
   Feeling like you have control over your work is another important factor for intrinsic motivation. People are naturally more motivated when they have the freedom to make decisions about how they complete their tasks. Jobs that offer autonomy—whether it's flexible hours, the ability to work from home, or having a say in decision-making—tend to foster higher levels of motivation. When people feel trusted and empowered, they are more likely to take ownership of their work and give their best effort.

The Balance Between External and Internal Factors

In reality, work motivation is a balance between external and internal factors. While it's tempting to focus on things like salary and job perks, true motivation often comes from a deeper source. It's about finding meaning in what we do, feeling supported and recognised, and having opportunities to grow. When these elements align, we're more likely to feel fulfilled—not just at work, but in life outside of work as well.

As we progress through this book, we'll continue to explore how these factors play out in real-life scenarios, offering practical tips and solutions for improving your work-life balance. By understanding what motivates us, we can take steps to create a work environment that supports both our professional and personal well-being.

Chapter 2: Well-being Within the Workplace

Imagine this: it's ten years from now, and workplace stress and burnout are still widespread problems. What would that tell us? It would reveal a failure on society's part to address an issue that has been recognised for decades. Despite all the discussions about mental health and work-life balance, many companies still don't prioritize their employees' well-being. Instead, they often focus on key performance indicators (KPIs), profits, and productivity, leaving well-being as an afterthought.

In recent years, there has been growing awareness of how toxic work environments can harm employees. Numerous studies have highlighted this issue. For example, one report found that 75% of UK employees have experienced some form of bullying or belittling at work. Another study by Champion Health revealed that toxic workplaces can lead to anxiety, depression, and decreased job satisfaction. These studies raise an important question: if we know toxic work environments are damaging, why are so many companies still failing to take employee well-being seriously?

The Problem with "Band-Aid" Solutions

One of the biggest issues is that many companies resort to quick fixes when it comes to improving employee well-being. They may set up a wellness program or offer a few mental health days, but these solutions often fail to address the deeper issues that cause stress and burnout in the first place. It's like putting a band-aid on a wound without treating the root cause.

For example, some companies offer yoga classes or meditation sessions as part of their wellness programs. While these activities can be helpful, they don't get to the heart of the problem. If employees are constantly overloaded with work, facing unrealistic targets, or dealing with poor leadership, no amount of yoga is going to fix that. In fact, these programs can sometimes feel like empty gestures if they aren't backed by real changes in the company's culture.

What companies really need to do is dig deeper and look at the root causes of stress and burnout. Heavy workloads, lack of communication, and poor management are often the true culprits. Addressing these issues means changing the way work is organised and ensuring that employees have the support they need to thrive.

Why a Healthy Work Environment Matters

A healthy work environment isn't just nice to have—it's essential for both employees and the company itself. When employees feel good about where they work, they are more motivated, more productive, and more likely to stick around. On the other hand, when people are constantly stressed or burned out, it affects not only their performance but also their mental and physical health. Long-term stress can lead to anxiety, depression, and even serious health issues like heart disease.

Companies that prioritise well-being tend to have lower employee turnover, higher engagement, and better overall performance. It's not just about being "nice" to employees; it's about creating an environment where people can perform at their best. When people feel supported and valued, they are far more likely to be engaged with their work and give their best effort.

The Impact of Leadership on Well-being

Leadership plays a crucial role in shaping the well-being of employees. A good leader can make all the difference between a toxic and a healthy workplace. Leaders who are empathetic, supportive, and open to feedback create an environment where employees feel safe and valued. On the flip side, poor leadership can quickly lead to a toxic environment.

For example, think about a manager who constantly micromanages their team, checks in every few minutes, and never trusts their employees to make decisions. Over time, this type of leadership can create a stressful environment where employees feel anxious and unable to perform at their best. Compare that to a leader who encourages their team to take ownership of their work, trusts them to make decisions, and offers guidance when needed. Employees in this type of environment are likely to feel more confident, motivated, and engaged.

One interesting study by Gallup found that employees who have supportive managers are more than twice as likely to be engaged in their work. This shows just how important leadership is when it comes to well-being. It's not enough to have wellness programs or mental health days; leaders need to actively create a culture where well-being is prioritised.

The Disconnect Between Company Priorities and Employee Well-being

One of the biggest problems in many companies today is the disconnect between what companies say they value and what they actually prioritise. Many organizations claim that they care about employee well-being, but when you look at how they operate, it's clear that profits and performance metrics come first. This disconnect creates frustration among employees, who may feel that their well-being is not truly valued.

For instance, a company might roll out a new wellness initiative but still expect employees to work long hours and meet unrealistic deadlines. In such cases, the wellness program feels like little more than a public relations move. Employees can see through these half-hearted efforts, and they may even feel resentful when the company claims to care about well-being while continuing to overload them with work.

To create real change, companies need to align their priorities with their values. If well-being is truly important, it should be reflected in every aspect of the workplace—from how work is assigned to how employees are treated by their managers. Companies need to make well-being a core part of their culture, not just something they talk about in staff meetings or use as a marketing tool.

Work-Life Balance: More Than Just a Trend

The idea of work-life balance has been a popular topic for years, but it's not just a trend—it's a fundamental part of creating a healthy workplace. People need time to rest, recharge, and spend with their loved ones. Without that balance, it's easy to feel burned out and disconnected from life outside of work.

A healthy work-life balance doesn't look the same for everyone. Some people thrive in fast-paced environments and enjoy working long hours, while others need more time to recharge. The key is for companies to recognise that every employee is different and to provide flexibility when it comes to work schedules and expectations.

For example, flexible working hours or remote work options can help employees find a better balance between work and personal life. When people have control over their time, they are more likely to feel satisfied and less stressed. Offering flexibility shows that the company respects employees' personal lives and trusts them to get their work done without strict oversight.

Creating a Culture of Well-being

Building a culture of well-being doesn't happen overnight. It requires a commitment from leadership, a willingness to listen to employees, and a real understanding of what drives stress and burnout in the workplace. Here are a few practical steps that companies can take to create a culture of well-being:

1. **Listen to Employees**
   The first step to improving well-being is listening. Employees know better than anyone what causes stress and burnout in their workplace. By creating open lines of communication, companies can gather valuable feedback and make changes that truly matter. This might mean setting up regular check-ins, conducting anonymous surveys, or creating forums where employees can voice their concerns.

2. **Promote Work-Life Balance**
   Encourage employees to take time off, disconnect from work after hours, and prioritise their personal lives. Offering flexible working arrangements and making sure people aren't overburdened with work are essential steps toward creating balance.

3. **Invest in Mental Health Resources**
   Offering mental health support—whether through counseling services, stress management workshops, or wellness programs—can make a big difference in helping employees manage stress. However, it's important that these resources go beyond surface-level solutions. Companies need to address the deeper issues causing stress, such as workload and leadership problems, to make real improvements.

4. **Lead by Example**
   Leadership needs to model the behaviors they want to see in their employees. This means taking breaks,

respecting work-life boundaries, and showing that well-being is a priority for everyone in the organisation.

By implementing these strategies, companies can create a workplace where people feel supported, valued, and motivated. When employees are well, both mentally and physically, the benefits extend far beyond individual well-being. The company as a whole thrives, with higher productivity, better employee retention, and a more positive work environment.

Chapter 3: A Journey to Purpose and Fulfillment

Gone are the days when society dictated what a career should look like. The traditional idea of a 9-to-5 job in a stable profession no longer holds the same appeal for everyone. More and more people are questioning the conventional career paths that were once seen as the only route to success. In today's world, many are searching for something deeper—something that brings them both fulfillment and purpose. This shift in mindset is changing the way we think about work, as people prioritise personal growth, creativity, and happiness over simply earning a paycheck.

For decades, society emphasised stability. People were encouraged to follow the same path: get an education, find a secure job, work hard, and eventually retire. While there's nothing inherently wrong with that approach, it doesn't work for everyone. As the world evolves and industries change, people are discovering new ways to build careers that align with their passions and values. We are living in an age of globalisation and digitisation, where the rise of technology has opened the door to a wide range of new career options—many of which didn't exist just a few decades ago.

The Impact of Digital Innovation on Career Paths

One of the most significant changes in recent years is the rise of digital careers. The internet has transformed the way we work, giving rise to professions that were unimaginable a few decades ago. Jobs like content creators, bloggers, influencers, virtual assistants, and online educators have become mainstream. These new-age careers offer people the freedom to design their lives around their interests and passions, breaking free from the constraints of traditional office jobs.

Consider the story of Adrian, an artist who turned his passion into a successful career. As a young boy, Adrian loved to draw. His talent was evident early on, and his friends began asking him to draw portraits for them. Eventually, Adrian realised that he could make money doing what he loved. He started a small business selling his artwork, and over time, it grew into something much bigger. Today, Adrian is a well-known artist whose work has been featured in films and galleries around the world. His story is a powerful reminder that passion, when combined with hard work and perseverance, can lead to incredible success.

Adrian's journey highlights a growing trend: people are no longer content to follow the traditional paths laid out for them by society. They want careers that bring them joy, challenge them, and allow them to express their creativity. Whether it's through online platforms, freelance work, or entrepreneurship, people are finding new ways to turn their passions into fulfilling careers.

Finding Purpose in a Changing World

As the career landscape changes, so too does our understanding of what it means to have a fulfilling career. For many, work is no longer just a means to an end—it's a way to express who they are and what they believe in. People are looking for jobs that align with their values, whether it's through meaningful work, contributing to a greater cause, or simply enjoying the creative process.

Take the example of content creators and influencers. A decade ago, few would have imagined that people could build successful careers by sharing their thoughts, ideas, and creative projects with the world. Today, many people have done just that, using platforms like YouTube, Instagram, and TikTok to create content that resonates with millions of viewers. For these individuals, the goal isn't just financial success—it's about connecting with their audience, sharing their passions, and making a positive impact on others.

What makes these careers so appealing is that they allow people to pursue their interests on their own terms. They are no longer tied to the expectations of a traditional job or the limitations of a fixed work schedule. Instead, they have the freedom to design their own lives, often finding greater fulfillment in the process.

The Importance of Self-Discovery

In this age of endless opportunities, many people are discovering that finding purpose in their work isn't about following someone else's path—it's about creating their own. Self-discovery plays a crucial role in this journey. To truly find fulfillment, we need to take the time to explore our interests, understand our values, and identify what brings us joy. This isn't always an easy process, but it's one that is deeply rewarding.

For many people, the biggest challenge is overcoming the pressure to conform to societal expectations. From a young age, we're taught to pursue stability and security, often at the expense of our passions. Society tells us that success means getting a "good job," making a lot of money, and climbing the corporate ladder. But what happens when that path doesn't align with who we are?

This is where the journey of self-discovery comes in. It's about questioning the conventional wisdom and asking ourselves what we really want out of life. It's about finding the courage to step outside of our comfort zones and pursue the things that truly matter to us. Whether that means changing careers, starting a business, or simply exploring a new hobby, self-discovery is the key to finding purpose and fulfillment.

The Role of Passion in Career Fulfillment

Passion is the fuel that drives us toward meaningful work. When we are passionate about what we do, we feel energised, motivated, and excited to tackle new challenges. Passion transforms work from a mundane task into something that brings joy and satisfaction. It's the reason why some people are willing to wake up at 4 a.m. to pursue their goals, while others dread the start of the workday.

Finding a career that aligns with our passions isn't always easy, but it's worth the effort. Think about the difference between someone who works purely for the paycheque and someone who is deeply invested in their work because it excites them. The latter is more likely to feel fulfilled, to go the extra mile, and to find meaning in their daily tasks. They aren't just working to earn a living—they're working because they genuinely enjoy what they do.

However, passion alone isn't enough. It needs to be paired with hard work, perseverance, and a willingness to take risks. Turning a passion into a successful career often requires stepping outside of the traditional boundaries and embracing new ways of thinking. It may mean starting from scratch, learning new skills, or taking on challenges that seem daunting at first. But for those who are willing to take the leap, the rewards can be life-changing.

Overcoming External and Societal Pressures

One of the biggest obstacles to finding fulfillment in our careers is the pressure to conform to societal expectations. From a young age, we're told what success should look like, and it often doesn't leave much room for creativity or personal exploration.

We're expected to follow a certain path—go to school, get a good job, and stick with it, even if it doesn't bring us happiness.

Breaking free from these expectations can be difficult, but it's essential if we want to find true fulfillment. This means letting go of the fear of judgment or failure and focusing on what matters to us personally. It's about trusting our instincts and following our passions, even when the path ahead isn't clear.

For some, this might mean leaving a stable job to pursue a dream, like starting a business or changing careers. For others, it might mean finding ways to make their current job more meaningful by taking on new challenges or projects that align with their interests. Whatever the case may be, the key is to stay true to yourself and not be afraid to redefine what success looks like for you.

The Journey is Just as Important as the Destination

Finding purpose and fulfillment in your career is a journey, not a destination. Along the way, there will be challenges, setbacks, and moments of doubt. But these are all part of the process. The important thing is to keep moving forward, to stay open to new opportunities, and to continue learning about yourself and what makes you happy.

Sometimes, the journey itself is more valuable than the destination. Each experience, whether it's a success or a failure, teaches us something new about ourselves and helps us grow. By embracing the journey and remaining open to change, we can create a career that not only provides for us financially but also brings joy, purpose, and fulfillment.

Chapter 4: An Obsession with Being Busy

One of the biggest frustrations in modern life is feeling like there's never enough time. We are constantly juggling work, family, social commitments, and personal interests. Time is one of our most precious resources—free to use but impossible to hold onto. As motivational speaker Jim Rohn once said, "Either you run the day, or the day runs you." But for many people, it often feels like the day runs them, with little time left to stop and catch their breath.

Our obsession with being busy has become a badge of honour in today's society. People wear their packed schedules like a mark of success, as though being constantly in motion proves that they are productive and valuable. But in reality, this busyness often comes at the expense of our well-being. We rush from one task to the next, leaving little room to relax, reflect, or simply enjoy the moment. As a result, we are left feeling exhausted, disconnected from ourselves and those around us.

In this chapter, we will explore how our obsession with being busy has become ingrained in modern life, why it's so difficult to slow down, and how we can reclaim our time and our peace of mind.

The Illusion of Busyness: Are We Really That Busy?

On the surface, it seems like everyone is busier than ever. People complain about having too much to do and not enough hours in the day. But is it true? Are we genuinely busier than past generations, or has our perception of time changed?

In many ways, the pace of life has accelerated, thanks in large part to technology. We are constantly connected—our phones buzz with notifications, emails demand immediate responses, and social media keeps us engaged around the clock. The pressure to stay connected, both socially and professionally, makes it feel like we are always "on." Even our downtime is often filled with distractions, as we check our phones or scroll through endless streams of information. This gives us the impression that we are constantly busy, even when we're not actually accomplishing much.

The reality is, we all have the same 24 hours in a day, just like previous generations. What has changed is how we use and perceive that time. In the past, people may have been just as busy, but they didn't have the same level of constant stimulation and pressure to be available at all times. Today, we have become so accustomed to multitasking and filling every moment with activity that the idea of doing "nothing" feels uncomfortable, even impossible.

The Downside of Being Too Busy

While being busy might make us feel productive, it can have serious downsides for both our mental and physical health. The constant rush to get things done leaves little room for rest, relaxation, or meaningful reflection. When we are too busy, we often become disconnected from our own thoughts and emotions, as well as from the people around us.

One of the biggest consequences of busyness is burnout. Many people push themselves to the limit, juggling work, family, and personal obligations without taking the time to recharge. This can lead to chronic stress, fatigue, and even physical health problems like heart disease and high blood pressure. Emotionally, constant busyness can lead to feelings of anxiety, frustration, and a sense of being overwhelmed.

Another downside of busyness is that it often prevents us from enjoying the present moment. Instead of savoring our experiences, we rush through them, always thinking about the next thing on our to-do list. We might be physically present, but our minds are elsewhere, focused on what still needs to be done. As a result, we miss out on opportunities to connect with others and experience joy in the little moments of life.

Why Do We Stay So Busy?

If being busy is so draining, why do we stay so caught up in it? There are a few reasons why busyness has become so ingrained in our culture.

1. **Social Pressure**
   In many societies, being busy is seen as a sign of success. People equate having a full schedule with being important, productive, and successful. This mindset has become so widespread that not being busy can sometimes feel like a failure. If we're not constantly working or achieving something, we might worry that we're falling behind or not living up to expectations.

Social media has only amplified this pressure. People often post about their busy lives, showing off their packed calendars, accomplishments, and work-related successes. This creates a culture of comparison, where we feel like we need to keep up with others, even if it means sacrificing our own well-being.

2. **Avoiding Discomfort**
   Busyness can also be a way to avoid facing uncomfortable thoughts or emotions. When we're constantly in motion, there's little time for self-reflection or dealing with underlying issues. Some people use busyness as a distraction, keeping themselves occupied to avoid confronting problems in their personal lives, relationships, or mental health. It's easier to stay busy than to face difficult emotions or make changes.

3. **Fear of Missing Out (FOMO)**
   The fear of missing out, or FOMO, is another reason why people stay busy. We don't want to miss out on opportunities, whether they are social, professional, or personal. As a result, we say "yes" to too many things, overcommit ourselves, and end up stretched too thin. This can lead to a cycle of busyness that's hard to break, as we feel pressured to do more and more, even when we're already overwhelmed.

The Importance of Slowing Down

While it might seem impossible to slow down in today's fast-paced world, it's essential for our mental, emotional, and physical well-being. Slowing down allows us to reconnect with ourselves, reduce stress, and find more meaning in our daily lives.

Here are a few reasons why slowing down is so important:

1. **Mental Clarity and Focus**
   When we're constantly rushing from one task to the next, it's hard to think clearly. Slowing down gives us the space to reflect, prioritise, and make better decisions. It allows us to focus on what truly matters, rather than getting caught up in the noise of daily life.

2. **Emotional Well-being**
   Taking time to rest and recharge is crucial for emotional well-being. Slowing down helps reduce stress, anxiety, and the risk of burnout. It also gives us the opportunity to process our emotions and gain perspective on challenges we might be facing.

3. **Building Deeper Connections**
   When we're less busy, we have more time to connect with the people who matter most. Whether it's

spending quality time with family and friends or simply being present in our relationships, slowing down allows us to nurture deeper, more meaningful connections.

How to Reclaim Your Time

If you're feeling overwhelmed by busyness, it's important to take steps to reclaim your time and create more balance in your life. Here are a few practical ways to do this:

1. **Set Boundaries**
   One of the most effective ways to reduce busyness is to set clear boundaries around your time. This might mean saying "no" to certain commitments or limiting the amount of time you spend on work outside of office hours. It's okay to prioritise your own well-being and protect your time.

2. **Schedule Downtime**
   Just as you schedule meetings and appointments, schedule time for rest and relaxation. Make it a priority to set aside moments in your day where you can unwind, disconnect from technology, and simply be present. Whether it's taking a walk in nature, reading a book, or practicing mindfulness, having dedicated downtime can help restore balance.

3. **Focus on What Matters**
   Rather than trying to do everything, focus on the tasks and activities that truly matter to you. What brings you joy? What aligns with your values and long-term goals? By prioritising these things, you can reduce the clutter in your schedule and create more space for the things that are most important.

4. **Practice Mindfulness**
   Mindfulness is a powerful tool for slowing down and

staying present in the moment. Whether it's through meditation, deep breathing, or simply paying attention to your thoughts and feelings, mindfulness can help you break the cycle of busyness and find more peace in your daily life.

Conclusion: The Power of Doing Less

In a world that celebrates busyness, it can feel counterintuitive to slow down. But the truth is, doing less doesn't mean you're less successful or productive. In fact, it often leads to greater clarity, more meaningful connections, and a deeper sense of fulfillment. By taking control of your time and focusing on what truly matters, you can break free from the cycle of busyness and create a life that feels balanced, peaceful, and full of purpose.

Chapter 5: Seeing the Journey Ahead of the Crossroad

Life is full of crossroads—moments where we have to make tough decisions that can change the direction of our future. These moments often come unexpectedly, whether it's a career crisis, a personal challenge, or an unforeseen event that forces us to pause and reevaluate our next steps. At these crossroads, our ability to think clearly and make decisions can be tested, and how we respond to them can shape the rest of our journey.

We rarely think about these crossroads until we're standing right in front of them. When the pressure is on, it's easy to feel overwhelmed, and many of us struggle to know what to do. The challenge lies not just in making the decision, but in having the foresight and strategy to navigate through the obstacles that come our way. Some people seem to handle these situations with ease, remaining calm, focused, and collected, while others may panic or feel stuck, unsure of what to do next.

In this chapter, we'll explore how to anticipate and prepare for these pivotal moments, and how a thoughtful approach to decision-making can make all the difference. The ability to plan ahead, remain composed, and think strategically is key to overcoming life's challenges.

Anticipating the Crossroad: Strategy and Preparation

One of the best ways to handle a crossroad is to anticipate it before it arrives. Life may be full of surprises, but that doesn't mean we can't be prepared for the unexpected. Successful people often seem like they're always two steps ahead, able to navigate challenges with ease. This isn't because they're lucky—it's because they've developed strategies to manage both expected and unexpected events.

Take, for example, the game of chess. In chess, each move you make is a calculated decision based on where the pieces are and where they could be in the future. A good chess player isn't just thinking about their next move—they're thinking several moves ahead, anticipating how their opponent will respond, and planning their strategy accordingly. Life works in much the same way. By thinking ahead and preparing for possible outcomes, we can approach our crossroads with confidence, knowing we've considered the possibilities.

A key part of this preparation is building a personal toolkit of skills and strategies that help you stay organised and focused when the time comes to make a decision. These tools include staying calm under pressure, seeking advice from others, weighing the pros and cons, and learning from past experiences. Successful people aren't necessarily more talented or intelligent—they've simply learned how to make decisions thoughtfully and strategically.

The Power of Calm and Composure

When we find ourselves at a crossroad, one of the most important qualities we can have is composure. Remaining calm in the face of uncertainty allows us to think more clearly and make better decisions. Unfortunately, many people struggle to stay calm during high-pressure moments, letting stress or panic cloud their judgment. But just like any other skill, maintaining composure can be learned and practiced.

Some years ago, I worked at a school in East London where I saw firsthand how calm leadership can diffuse even the most difficult situations. One day, an upset parent stormed into the school, ready to confront a teacher about an issue with her child. The parent was visibly angry, raising her voice and demanding immediate action. The headteacher, upon hearing the commotion, approached the situation with incredible calmness. She greeted the parent warmly and invited her to a private office, away from the chaos of the hallway. By the time they reemerged, the situation had been resolved, and the once-irate parent was smiling and thankful.

This incident is a powerful reminder of the importance of calmness and composure in moments of crisis. Staying calm allows us to see the bigger picture and find solutions that we might not have considered otherwise. When we panic or act out of fear, we often make hasty decisions that don't serve us in the long run. By remaining composed, we give ourselves the space to think clearly and respond thoughtfully.

Strategic Decision-Making: Head vs. Heart

One of the toughest aspects of decision-making is the struggle between head and heart. Should we make decisions based on logic and reason, or should we follow our gut instincts and emotions? The answer is often a delicate balance between the two. Both logic and emotion play important roles in our decision-making process, and learning when to rely on each can help us make better choices.

On one hand, logic provides us with a clear, structured way to analyse a situation. It helps us weigh the pros and cons, consider the long-term consequences, and make decisions based on facts and evidence. Logic is especially useful when we need to make practical decisions, such as choosing a career path, making financial choices, or solving problems that require a rational approach.

On the other hand, our emotions give us valuable insight into what truly matters to us. When we follow our heart, we tap into our passions, values, and desires. Emotional decision-making is important when it comes to personal relationships, creative pursuits, and situations where our feelings play a key role in our happiness.

The key is finding the right balance between head and heart. Too much logic can lead to cold, calculated decisions that lack passion or purpose. Too much emotion can cause us to act impulsively or make decisions that don't serve us in the long run. By considering both the logical and emotional aspects of a decision, we can make choices that are not only practical but also aligned with our values and desires.

Breaking Down Decisions Into Manageable Steps

One of the reasons crossroads feel so overwhelming is that we often view them as all-or-nothing situations. We think we need to have all the answers immediately, and that any wrong move could lead to failure. But in reality, most decisions aren't as drastic as they seem. By breaking them down into smaller, manageable steps, we can make the process feel less daunting and more achievable.

Think of it like building a bridge. You don't need to know every detail of how the bridge will look when it's finished—you just need to lay one brick at a time. Similarly, when faced with a tough decision, focus on the first step you can take. Once that step is complete, move on to the next one. This approach not only makes the decision-making process more manageable but also allows you to adjust your course as new information becomes available.

Successful people understand the value of taking small, deliberate steps toward their goals. They don't rush into decisions or try to solve everything at once. Instead, they break down the problem, tackle each part methodically, and build momentum over time.

Learning From Past Experiences

Our past experiences are some of the most valuable tools we have when it comes to navigating life's crossroads. Every decision we've made, whether it was a success or a failure, teaches us something important about how we handle challenges. By reflecting on our past decisions, we can identify patterns in our thinking, learn from our mistakes, and apply those lessons to future situations.

For example, think about a time when you faced a difficult decision and made the wrong choice. What went wrong? Were you too impulsive? Did you fail to gather enough information? Or perhaps you ignored your gut instincts in favor of what seemed logical at the time. By analysing these past decisions, you can better understand your decision-making style and make more informed choices in the future.

On the flip side, reflecting on your successes can help reinforce positive decision-making habits. What worked well in the past? How did you stay calm under pressure? What strategies did you use to think through the problem? By focusing on what went right, you can build confidence in your ability to handle future challenges.

Seeing Beyond the Crossroad

At the end of the day, every crossroad is an opportunity for growth. While it might feel overwhelming in the moment, each decision you make brings you one step closer to your goals. It's important to remember that there is no "perfect" decision—every path has its challenges and rewards. The key is to approach each crossroad with a clear mind, a thoughtful strategy, and the confidence that you have the tools to navigate whatever comes your way.

By planning ahead, staying calm under pressure, and learning from your past experiences, you can make informed decisions that lead to personal and professional growth. Whether the challenge is big or small, the ability to see the journey ahead and take deliberate steps toward your goals is what will ultimately lead to success.

Chapter 6: Beyond the Salary: What Would Get You Out of Bed at 4 a.m.?

Let's be honest—most of us work because we need to make a living. Money is important. It pays the bills, puts food on the table, and gives us a sense of security. But deep down, we know that money alone isn't enough to bring true fulfillment. If it were, everyone with a high salary would be thrilled with their lives, and we know that's not the case. So, what is it that really gets us out of bed every morning? What keeps us motivated, even when the alarm rings at 4 a.m., and we could easily roll over and go back to sleep?

In this chapter, we'll explore the idea that fulfillment at work goes far beyond just earning a paycheque. We'll look at the deeper reasons why people wake up every day feeling excited about what they do, and why finding purpose in our work can make all the difference between feeling stuck and feeling alive.

The Limitations of Money as Motivation

There's no doubt that having financial stability is important. A decent salary provides a sense of security and allows us to meet our basic needs. But when we rely solely on money as our motivation for going to work, we often find ourselves feeling empty, stressed, or even burned out. Why? Because no matter how much money we make, if our work lacks meaning or doesn't align with our values, we're likely to feel unfulfilled in the long run.

Think about it: How many people have you heard say, "I'm only doing this job for the money"? It's a common sentiment, and while it's understandable, it's not sustainable. Eventually, the long hours, the stress, and the lack of purpose catch up with us.

We start to dread going to work, and even a big paycheque doesn't feel worth it anymore.

On the other hand, people who find fulfillment in their work tend to wake up with a sense of purpose, whether they're earning a lot of money or not. For them, it's not just about the salary—it's about doing something that matters, something that excites them and makes them feel like they're contributing to something bigger.

What Drives Us Beyond the Paycheck?

So, if money isn't enough to motivate us in the long term, what is? The answer often lies in what gives us a sense of **purpose** and **passion**. When we feel like our work has meaning, it energises us in a way that money alone cannot. Here are a few reasons why people find themselves motivated to get up and face the day, even when their salary isn't the primary driver:

1. **A Sense of Purpose**
   Finding purpose in your work is one of the most powerful motivators there is. Purpose goes beyond the daily tasks and responsibilities; it's about feeling like what you're doing matters. Whether it's helping others, solving a problem, or contributing to a cause, having a sense of purpose can give you the energy to keep going, even when the work gets tough.

Think of people in jobs that aren't always glamorous but have a deep sense of purpose behind them—teachers who shape young minds, healthcare workers who save lives, or social workers who help vulnerable communities. These people don't wake up early every day just for a paycheck. They do it because they believe in the impact of their work. Their motivation comes from the knowledge that they're making a difference, even if it's in small ways.

2. **Passion for What You Do**
   When you're passionate about your work, it doesn't feel like a chore. Instead, it becomes something you look forward to, something that excites you and keeps you engaged. Passionate people often talk about how they lose track of time when they're working—whether they're writing, designing, building, or teaching, they're fully immersed in what they do because it's something they genuinely enjoy.

Take Adrian, the artist we mentioned earlier. He found his passion for drawing at a young age, and as he grew older, he turned that passion into a thriving career. Adrian wakes up excited about his work, not because he's chasing financial success, but because he loves what he does. His art gives him a sense of purpose and joy that no paycheque could ever replace.

3. **Personal Growth and Development**
   Another key motivator is the opportunity for personal growth. When our work challenges us and helps us develop new skills, we feel a sense of accomplishment that goes beyond financial reward. Whether it's learning a new technique, mastering a difficult task, or taking on a leadership role, personal growth gives us the confidence and motivation to keep moving forward.

Consider someone who starts a new job that pushes them out of their comfort zone. At first, they might feel nervous or overwhelmed, but as they start to learn and grow, they gain a sense of pride in their progress. That feeling of development can be incredibly motivating, and it's often the reason people stick with challenging jobs—they know they're growing, both personally and professionally.

4. **Making an Impact**
   Feeling like you're making an impact is another

powerful motivator. It's the idea that your work is contributing to something larger than yourself. For some people, this impact might be felt on a small scale—like helping a customer solve a problem or supporting a colleague through a tough day. For others, the impact might be larger—like working on a project that helps a community or developing a product that changes people's lives.

When we feel like our work has an impact, it becomes more than just a job—it becomes a way to leave a mark on the world. This sense of contribution can be deeply fulfilling, giving us a reason to get up and give our best, even on days when the work is hard.

What Would Get You Out of Bed at 4 a.m.?

Now, let's bring it back to you. Think about what really motivates you. If money weren't an issue, what would get you out of bed at 4 a.m. with excitement? What would make you eager to start your day, even before the sun comes up?

For some, the answer might be a creative pursuit—writing, painting, or playing music. For others, it might be a cause they're passionate about, like environmental advocacy, social justice, or helping others in need. Still, others might be driven by a desire to grow and learn, to take on new challenges and become the best version of themselves.

It's important to reflect on what truly matters to you, because that's where you'll find the deeper motivation that goes beyond the paycheque. If you're doing work that aligns with your passions, your values, and your sense of purpose, you'll find that getting up in the morning feels less like a chore and more like an opportunity.

Aligning Your Work With Your Values

Once you've identified what motivates you, the next step is to align your work with those values. This doesn't always mean making a drastic career change—sometimes, it's about finding ways to bring more of what you love into your current job. Maybe you can take on projects that allow you to use your creative skills, or perhaps you can find ways to mentor others and help them grow.

It's also important to remember that not every job will be perfect, and that's okay. But if you can find ways to incorporate your passions and values into your work, you'll likely feel more fulfilled, even if the job itself isn't your dream career.

When It's Time to Make a Change

Of course, there are times when our current job just doesn't align with what we truly want. If you find yourself feeling drained, unmotivated, or disconnected from your work, it might be time to consider a change. This doesn't mean you have to quit your job immediately—sometimes, it's about taking small steps toward a new path.

Maybe you start exploring other career options, take a class to learn a new skill, or begin working on a side project that excites you. The key is to stay open to new possibilities and trust that finding work that aligns with your values is possible.

Conclusion: Beyond the Salary

At the end of the day, the real question isn't just "What will get you out of bed in the morning?"—it's "What will keep you motivated and fulfilled over the long haul?" Money is important, but it's only part of the equation. True fulfillment comes from doing work that aligns with your values, brings you joy, and allows you to make an impact.

When you find that kind of work—whether it's in your current job or a future career—you'll know it. It's the kind of work that doesn't just get you out of bed at 4 a.m.; it's the kind of work that makes you excited to face the day, knowing that what you do matters.

Chapter 7: The Art of Switching Off

In today's hectic, hyper-connected world, we are always "on." From the moment we wake up to the moment we fall asleep, our minds are constantly racing. Emails, social media, work tasks, news alerts—it never stops. We've become a generation that equates busyness with success, making the idea of sitting still or switching off feel almost impossible. But deep down, we all know that living in a constant state of motion isn't healthy. The real challenge is finding ways to switch off in a world that never seems to slow down.

The art of switching off isn't just about stepping away from work. It's about giving yourself permission to disconnect from the chaos of modern life, to find moments of peace and stillness that help you recharge and reconnect with yourself. In this chapter, we'll explore why switching off is so important for our mental and emotional well-being, and how we can build habits that help us find calm amidst the noise.

The Noise of Modern Life: Why We Struggle to Switch Off

If you've ever felt overwhelmed by the constant demands of everyday life, you're not alone. The truth is, we are living in an age of information overload. Our brains are bombarded with stimuli all day, every day. Whether it's the buzz of your phone, the pressure to meet deadlines, or the endless stream of social media updates, it feels like there's always something demanding our attention.

It's no wonder so many of us struggle to switch off. Even when we do manage to step away from work, we often find ourselves filling that time with other forms of stimulation—scrolling through our phones, watching TV, or mentally running through our to-do list. We've become so accustomed to being constantly engaged that the idea of doing "nothing" can feel uncomfortable or even anxiety-inducing.

But switching off isn't about doing nothing—it's about being present. It's about creating space in your day to unwind, reflect, and simply be. The problem is, many of us have forgotten how to do that. We're so used to multitasking and filling every moment with activity that we've lost touch with the quiet moments that help us recharge.

The Consequences of Not Switching Off

Living in a constant state of busyness comes with a cost. When we don't take time to switch off, we risk burning out—both mentally and physically. Chronic stress from constantly being "on" can lead to a range of issues, from anxiety and depression to sleep problems and weakened immune systems. Over time, this can take a serious toll on our overall well-being.

But the consequences aren't just physical. When we don't switch off, we lose our ability to be present in the moment. Instead of fully enjoying time with loved ones, we're mentally checked out, thinking about work or distracted by our phones. We may be there physically, but our minds are elsewhere. This disconnect can prevent us from forming deeper connections and fully experiencing the joy of life's little moments.

Perhaps the most significant consequence of not switching off is that we lose touch with ourselves. When we're constantly moving from one task to the next, we don't have time to reflect on our feelings, our needs, or our desires. We become so focused on external demands that we forget to check in with what's going on inside.

Why Switching Off Matters

Switching off isn't a luxury—it's a necessity for our mental, emotional, and physical health. Taking time to unplug from the constant noise allows us to recharge, regain focus, and reconnect with ourselves and the world around us.

Here are a few reasons why switching off is so important:

1. **Mental Clarity and Focus**
   Our brains aren't designed to be in a state of constant stimulation. When we're always busy or distracted, it's harder to focus, think clearly, or make decisions. By taking time to switch off, we give our minds a chance to rest and reset, which in turn helps improve our mental clarity and focus.

2. **Emotional Well-Being**
   Switching off allows us to reconnect with our emotions. When we're constantly moving, we often push aside our feelings or distract ourselves from difficult emotions. But taking time to slow down and reflect helps us process those emotions, leading to greater emotional balance and well-being.

3. **Rest and Recovery**
   Just like our bodies need rest after physical activity, our minds need rest after long periods of mental activity. Switching off helps reduce stress, lower anxiety, and prevent burnout. It's a way to recharge our batteries so that we can approach life with renewed energy and focus.

4. **Being Present**
   In a world that's always demanding our attention, switching off helps us be more present. Whether it's enjoying time with family, taking a walk in nature, or simply savoring a quiet moment with a cup of tea, being

present allows us to fully experience life's moments and build deeper connections with ourselves and others.

Finding Moments of Calm: How to Switch Off in a Busy World

Switching off doesn't have to mean completely disconnecting from the world for days at a time (though that can be helpful too!). In fact, the art of switching off is about finding small moments of calm throughout your day—moments where you can step away from the noise, breathe, and give yourself space to unwind.

Here are a few simple ways to build the habit of switching off:

1. **Create Tech-Free Zones**
   One of the easiest ways to switch off is by setting boundaries around your use of technology. Consider creating tech-free zones in your home—like the bedroom or the dining table—where you can unplug from devices and focus on being present. These zones can become a safe space where you can recharge without the distractions of screens or notifications.

2. **Schedule Breaks for Mindfulness or Relaxation**
   Just like you schedule meetings or tasks, schedule time for yourself to relax. It doesn't have to be anything elaborate—just 10 to 15 minutes where you step away from work, sit quietly, or engage in mindfulness practices like meditation or deep breathing. Even a short break can help reset your mind and reduce stress.

3. **Take a Walk in Nature**
   There's something incredibly soothing about spending time in nature. Whether it's a park, a forest, or a simple neighbourhood walk, being outdoors helps us disconnect from the hustle and reconnect with the natural world. Research has shown that spending time

in nature can reduce stress, improve mood, and even enhance creativity. The next time you feel overwhelmed, consider stepping outside for a few minutes to clear your mind.

4. **Practice Mindful Breathing**
   One of the quickest ways to switch off is through mindful breathing. When you're feeling stressed or overwhelmed, take a few moments to focus on your breath. Breathe in slowly for a count of four, hold for four, then exhale for four. This simple practice helps calm your nervous system and brings your mind back to the present moment.

5. **Set Boundaries Around Work**
   It's easy to let work spill into every part of our lives, especially if we're working from home or have a demanding job. But setting clear boundaries around when and how you work can help create a healthier work-life balance. Try to avoid checking emails or taking work calls outside of designated work hours, and give yourself permission to fully disconnect at the end of the day.

Learning to Embrace Stillness

At first, switching off might feel uncomfortable, especially if you're used to being constantly busy. Stillness can feel strange, even anxiety-provoking, because it forces us to sit with our thoughts and feelings. But the more you practice switching off, the more you'll learn to embrace those quiet moments and appreciate the peace they bring.

Think of switching off like hitting the reset button on your mind and body. It's a chance to step back, breathe, and reconnect with yourself. It's a way to recharge so that you can face the world with greater clarity and calm.

The Art of Balancing Busyness and Calm

In a world that celebrates busyness, it can feel counterintuitive to switch off. But the truth is, balance is the key to long-term success and well-being. We can't function at our best if we're always running on empty. By learning the art of switching off, we give ourselves the space to recharge, refocus, and be more present in both our work and personal lives.

The next time you find yourself feeling overwhelmed by the constant demands of life, remember that it's okay to take a step back. It's okay to unplug, slow down, and take a moment for yourself. In fact, it's essential. The world will keep spinning, but you deserve the peace that comes from switching off and finding balance in a busy world.

Chapter 8: Lived Experiences Can Widen the Perspective

Everyone has a story, and no two stories are the same. Each of us goes through life collecting experiences—some good, some bad—that shape who we are and how we see the world. These lived experiences aren't just moments in time; they are the building blocks of our personal growth, influencing everything from the decisions we make to the way we approach challenges at work and in life.

In this chapter, we'll explore how our experiences, both personal and professional, play a key role in shaping our perspective. We'll dive into why it's important to embrace these experiences, learn from them, and use them to broaden our understanding of the world around us.

The Power of Lived Experience: Shaping Who We Are

We've all heard the saying, "Experience is the best teacher," and there's a lot of truth to that. No amount of formal education or theoretical knowledge can compare to the lessons we learn from real-life experiences. These moments—whether they involve successes, failures, challenges, or unexpected opportunities—help us grow in ways we couldn't have predicted.

Take a moment to think about some of the most defining experiences in your life. Maybe it was your first job, the time you travelled to a new place, or a difficult situation you had to navigate. Whatever it was, those experiences likely taught you something important—whether it was resilience, adaptability, patience, or empathy.

It's these experiences that shape our mindset and influence the way we approach our work, our relationships, and even our personal goals. For example, someone who has faced hardship may develop a stronger sense of empathy and patience, qualities that can be incredibly valuable in a work setting. On the other hand, someone who has travelled extensively may have gained a deeper appreciation for different cultures and perspectives, making them more open-minded and adaptable.

Embracing Both Good and Bad Experiences

It's easy to appreciate the good experiences in life—the ones that bring us joy, success, or personal fulfillment. But what about the tough times? The truth is, our most difficult experiences often offer the most valuable lessons. While it's natural to want to avoid pain or discomfort, it's during these challenging moments that we grow the most.

Consider someone who has faced a significant setback at work, like losing a job or failing to meet a big goal. In the moment, it's easy to feel defeated or discouraged. But when we look back on those experiences, we often realise that they were opportunities for growth. Maybe losing that job opened the door to a new career path, or maybe failing at something taught us to approach challenges differently next time.

Embracing both the good and bad experiences allows us to see life with more depth and perspective. Instead of viewing setbacks as failures, we can start to see them as stepping stones toward personal and professional growth. This mindset shift helps us become more resilient, adaptable, and confident in navigating whatever life throws our way.

How Lived Experiences Influence Our Work

Our lived experiences don't just shape us as individuals—they also influence the way we work. Whether we realise it or not, the lessons we've learned through our personal experiences often show up in our professional lives, helping us approach challenges with a more open and creative mindset.

For example, someone who has spent time volunteering or working in community-based roles might bring a strong sense of empathy and collaboration to the workplace. They're likely to approach teamwork with a greater understanding of how different perspectives and experiences can come together to create meaningful outcomes.

On the other hand, someone who has travelled the world or lived in different countries may have a unique ability to adapt to change and think outside the box. Their exposure to different cultures and ways of thinking makes them more likely to approach problems with creativity and flexibility, skills that are highly valuable in today's ever-changing work environments.

But it's not just the positive experiences that shape our work. Challenges, setbacks, and even failures teach us invaluable lessons about perseverance, problem-solving, and resilience. Someone who has faced tough situations—whether it's dealing with a difficult boss, overcoming financial struggles, or navigating a major life transition—has likely developed a stronger ability to handle stress and bounce back from adversity. These are the kinds of skills that can make a huge difference in the workplace, especially when things don't go as planned.

Broadening Our Perspective Through Diverse Experiences

One of the most powerful things about lived experiences is that they help us broaden our perspective. When we step outside of our comfort zones and experience something new—whether it's travelling to a different country, learning a new skill, or working with people from different backgrounds—we open ourselves up to new ways of thinking and seeing the world.

In today's globalised world, having a broad perspective is more important than ever. Being able to understand and appreciate different viewpoints makes us more empathetic, more adaptable, and more effective in both our personal and professional lives.

For example, someone who has worked in different industries or with diverse teams is more likely to approach problems with a flexible mindset. They understand that there's rarely one "right" way to do things, and they're open to exploring new ideas and solutions. This kind of adaptability is crucial in today's fast-paced work environments, where change is constant and innovation is key.

Similarly, someone who has spent time living or travelling abroad may have a deeper appreciation for cultural differences, making them more effective in collaborating with international teams or working in multicultural settings. Their lived experiences have given them the tools to navigate complex social dynamics and build stronger relationships with people from all walks of life.

Turning Experiences Into Wisdom

While experiences are powerful, they become even more valuable when we take the time to reflect on them. It's not enough to simply go through life collecting experiences—we need to pause, reflect, and extract the lessons they offer. This is how experiences turn into wisdom.

Reflection allows us to make sense of what we've been through and apply those lessons to future situations. It's the difference between someone who keeps repeating the same mistakes and someone who learns from their past and grows as a result.

Here are a few ways to turn your experiences into wisdom:

1. **Reflect Regularly**
   Take time to reflect on your experiences, both big and small. What did you learn? How did it shape you? What would you do differently next time? Reflection doesn't have to be formal—it can be as simple as taking a few minutes at the end of the day to think about what went well and what you could improve.

2. **Keep a Journal**
   Writing down your thoughts and reflections can be a powerful way to process your experiences. A journal allows you to track your growth over time and gives you a space to explore your thoughts and feelings in a deeper way.

3. **Seek Feedback**
   Sometimes, the people around us can offer valuable insights into our experiences. Ask for feedback from friends, family, or colleagues about how they've seen you grow or what they've observed in your approach to challenges. Their perspectives can help you see things you might have missed.

4. **Apply the Lessons**
   Wisdom comes from not just reflecting on your experiences but applying the lessons you've learned to future situations. When you face a new challenge, think back to similar experiences you've had in the past. How can you use what you've learned to make better decisions or approach the situation with more confidence?

The Value of Sharing Our Experiences

One of the most beautiful things about lived experiences is that they're meant to be shared. By opening up about our stories, we create connections with others and offer them the opportunity to learn from our journey. Whether it's through conversations, mentoring, or even writing, sharing our experiences helps others navigate their own paths.

It's important to remember that our experiences, no matter how personal, can have a universal impact. What you've been through might resonate with someone else, offering them guidance, support, or a new perspective. In sharing our stories, we not only help others but also gain a deeper understanding of ourselves.

Conclusion: A Life Rich with Experience

At the end of the day, our lived experiences are what make us who we are. They give us depth, wisdom, and the ability to see the world from a variety of perspectives. Whether good or bad, each experience offers a lesson that can help us grow and move forward in life with greater confidence and clarity.

Embracing the full spectrum of our experiences—both the highs and the lows—allows us to live a life that is rich with meaning. By reflecting on our past, learning from it, and sharing those lessons with others, we create a legacy of growth and resilience that can inspire those around us.

Conclusion: Designing Your Future on Your Own Terms

We've come a long way in this book, exploring the complexities of work-life balance, the challenges we face in our careers, and the importance of finding fulfillment beyond just earning a paycheck. Along the way, we've seen how our experiences—both personal and professional—shape who we are, how we approach work, and how we engage with the world around us.

One thing should be clear by now: while work is an important part of our lives, it doesn't have to define us. We are not bound by the traditional structures of work or societal expectations. Instead, we have the power to design our futures on our own terms. This doesn't mean that the journey is always easy, but it does mean that we have the freedom to make choices that align with our values, passions, and sense of purpose.

Taking Control of Your Journey

The road to fulfillment isn't about finding the "perfect" job or eliminating all stress from your life. It's about finding a balance that works for you—one that allows you to pursue meaningful work while also making time for the things that bring you joy outside of the office.

This might mean redefining what success looks like for you. Maybe it's not about climbing the corporate ladder or working endless hours for a bigger paycheck. Maybe it's about creating a life where work supports your personal goals, not the other way around. It's about making time for family, friends, and self-care, and recognizing that your worth isn't defined by your productivity or how busy you are.

Each of us is on our own unique journey, with our own set of challenges and aspirations. The key is to approach that journey with intention, knowing that you have the power to shape your future. Whether that means making small adjustments to your current work situation or taking a leap of faith into something new, the most important thing is that your choices reflect who you are and what truly matters to you.

Finding Meaning in the Everyday

One of the major themes in this book has been the search for meaning in our work and our lives. Finding fulfillment isn't always about making big changes—it's often about finding meaning in the everyday. It's about recognizing the small victories, the moments of connection, and the simple joys that make life richer.

Whether you're working a job that aligns with your passions or still searching for the right path, remember that meaning can be found in the present moment. It can be found in a conversation with a coworker, in the satisfaction of completing a task, or in the quiet moments when you step back and reflect on how far you've come.

When you approach life with a mindset of curiosity and gratitude, you open yourself up to new possibilities. You begin to see that even the challenges you face can offer valuable lessons that help you grow. And with each experience, your perspective widens, allowing you to approach your work and your life with greater clarity and confidence.

Redefining Success

Success isn't one-size-fits-all. It's deeply personal, and it's something we get to define for ourselves. For some, success might mean building a thriving career, while for others, it's about creating a life filled with adventure, creativity, or meaningful relationships. The important thing is that your definition of success reflects your values, not society's expectations.

In a world that often equates success with busyness and financial gain, it's easy to feel pressured to fit into a certain mold. But as we've explored in this book, true fulfillment comes when we listen to our own inner voice and pursue what makes us feel alive. Success is about finding balance, being present, and living in alignment with who you are.

The Power of Reflection and Growth

As we wrap up, one final lesson is worth remembering: growth is an ongoing process. The journey doesn't end once you've found your passion or achieved your goals. Life is constantly changing, and so are we. The key is to remain open to learning, to embrace new experiences, and to allow yourself to evolve over time.

Take time to reflect on your journey so far. What have you learned? How have you grown? What challenges have shaped you? And where do you want to go next? Reflection helps us make sense of our experiences and ensures that we continue to grow, no matter where we are in our careers or personal lives.

A Life on Your Own Terms

At the end of the day, the most important takeaway is this: you have the power to design a life that reflects who you are and what you value. You're not limited by what society expects of you or by the pressures of the modern workplace. You have the freedom to make choices that align with your passions, your goals, and your sense of purpose.

Whether you're seeking more balance in your current job, exploring new career paths, or simply trying to create more time for the things you love, remember that the journey is yours to shape. You have the power to take control of your future, to create a life that brings you both fulfillment and joy.

So, as you move forward, embrace the challenges, celebrate the victories, and always remember that you are in the driver's seat. The journey ahead is yours to design—on your own terms.

Printed in Great Britain
by Amazon